Celebrations in My World

Purim

Lynn
Peppas

Crabtree Publishing Company

www.crabtreebooks.com

Crabtree Publishing Company

www.crabtreebooks.com

Author: Lynn Peppas
Coordinating editor: Chester Fisher
Series editor: Susan LaBella
Subject Matter consultant: Rohail Aslam
Editor: Adrianna Morganelli
Proofreader: Molly Aloian
Editorial director: Kathy Middleton
Production coordinator: Katherine Berti
Prepress technician: Katherine Berti
Project manager: Kumar Kunal (Q2AMEDIA)
Art direction: Rahul Dhiman (Q2AMEDIA)
Cover design: Shruti Aggarwal (Q2AMEDIA)
Design: Cheena Yadav (Q2AMEDIA)
Photo research: Ekta Sharma (Q2AMEDIA)

Photographs:
AFP: Daoud Mizrahi: p. 27
Alamy: Israel Images: cover (main image); P. Gapper: p. 31
Associated Press: p. 30
Corbis: Annie Griffths Belt: p. 5, 17; Hanam Isachar: p. 29; Richard T. Nowitz:
    p. 18, 21
Dreamstime: Abasile: p. 7
Getty Images: Austrian School/ The Bridgeman Art Library: p. 9;
    Alfred Eisenstaedt/Time & Life Pictures: p. 25; Hermann Hnschuetz/
    The Bridgeman Art Library: p. 8; Mario Tama: p. 16
Istockphoto: David Joyner: p. 1, 28
Yair Karelic: p. 22, 23
PhotoEdit: Allan Oddie: p. 26
Photographers Direct: Gil Hidani: p. 19
PhotoStock-Israel: Llan D. Rosen: p. 20
Reuters: Gil Cohen Magen: p. 11; Stringer Russia: p. 6
Micheal J. Russell: p. 12
Shutterstock: cover (background); Mordechai Meiri: folio image, p. 10;
    Konstantin Sutyagin: p. 4
World Religions Photo Library: P. Gapper: p. 13, 14, 24; C. Osborne: p. 15

Library and Archives Canada Cataloguing in Publication

Peppas, Lynn
    Purim / Lynn Peppas.

(Celebrations in my world)
Includes index.
ISBN 978-0-7787-4764-2 (bound).--ISBN 978-0-7787-4782-6 (pbk.)

    1. Purim--Juvenile literature. I. Title.
II. Series: Celebrations in my world

BM695.P8P46 2009   j296.4'36   C2009-905188-5

Library of Congress Cataloging-in-Publication Data

Peppas, Lynn.
    Purim / Lynn Peppas.
        p. cm. -- (Celebrations in my world)
    Includes index.
    ISBN 978-0-7787-4782-6 (pbk. : alk. paper) -- ISBN 978-0-7787-4764-2
(reinforced library binding : alk. paper)
    1. Purim--Juvenile literature. I. Title. II. Series.

BM695.P8P465 2009
296.4'36--dc22

2009034809

0 325

Crabtree Publishing Company

www.crabtreebooks.com   1-800-387-7650

Printed in China/122009/CT20090915

Published in Canada
Crabtree Publishing
616 Welland Ave.
St. Catharines, ON
L2M 5V6

Published in the United States
Crabtree Publishing
350 Fifth Ave.
59th floor
New York, NY 10118

Published in the United Kingdom
Crabtree Publishing
Maritime House
Basin Road North, Hove
BN41 1WR

Published in Australia
Crabtree Publishing
386 Mt. Alexander Rd.
Ascot Vale (Melbourne)
VIC 3032

Contents

What is Purim?

Purim is a **religious** holiday. Jewish people celebrate it all around the world. It is a time to be happy and make others happy, too. Jewish people celebrate being saved from death thousands of years ago, by the courage of a young Jewish woman called Esther.

• Sunset is the time of day when the sun begins to go down in the sky.

DID YOU KNOW?

*All Jewish holidays begin and end at **sunset**. Purim is a one-day holiday. It begins at sunset and ends at sunset the next day.*

Jewish people
celebrate Purim.

Purim falls on different dates every year.
It happens in the springtime between
February and March. Jewish people
have a special religious **calendar**.
On the Jewish calendar, Purim always
falls in a month called Adar. Purim
is celebrated on the 14 of Adar.

What is Judaism?

Judaism is a religion that many Jewish people follow. Jewish people are often called Jews. Their **holy** book is the Torah. Religious leaders are called rabbis. Jews worship God in synagogues.

The Purim holiday is a happy time in synagogues.

DID YOU KNOW?

Jewish people speak many different languages today. Long ago, they spoke Hebrew. Many of their customs and holidays have Hebrew names.

A synagogue is a holy place where rabbis hold religious **services**. Today, Jewish people live all around the world. Many live in their homeland of Israel, too. Purim is a holiday celebrated in the synagogue and at home.

Hebrew letters look very different from our alphabet.

The Story of Esther

The Purim story comes from a Jewish book called the Megillah. The story took place thousands of years ago in Persia. Today, Persia is called Iran.

A woman named Esther was chosen by the King of Persia to be his queen. Esther's cousin Mordecai had once saved the king's life. The king was very grateful to him.

● Esther was a beautiful Jewish woman who became Queen of Persia.

One day, a man named Haman became angry at Mordecai. Mordecai was Jewish. So Haman convinced the king to let him kill all Jewish people. Esther revealed to the king that she was Jewish, too. She begged him to help her people. The king warned the Jews of Haman's plan. They beat their enemies, and Esther saved her people.

- The story of Esther is often written in Megillah scrolls like this one.

DID YOU KNOW?

Haman chose the day to kill all Jews by using a lottery. Pur is Hebrew for choosing by chance. The name Purim comes from Pur.

Listen to the Megillah

Jewish people are supposed to do four things during Purim. Listening to the Megillah is one of these. Other deeds to be done at Purim are to give to **charity**, give to others you know, and to share a big Purim **feast**.

On Purim, many Jewish people go to a synagogue.

• This gragger makes a lot of noise at Purim.

People are usually quiet during religious services but not on Purim. They listen to the Story of Esther in the Megillah. When Haman's name is read out loud people make a lot of noise. They stomp their feet. Some boo or hiss. They do this to drown out the sound of Haman's name.

These children make noise when they hear Haman's name read out loud.

Purim Charity

Giving to charity is another thing Jewish people do during Purim. Jewish people give to people who need it most. Even the poor are supposed to give gifts to others.

• People put money in charity boxes at the synagogue to help those in need.

DID YOU KNOW?

During Purim, Jewish people try to do "mitzvah." Mitzvah is the Hebrew word that means to do a good deed that God would like.

Jewish people give gifts
to those in need at Purim.

Gifts can be money, food, or clothing.
Every person in a family—even the
children—are supposed to give gifts
to the needy.

Gifts are to be given after reading the
Megillah. They should be given before
the Purim feast. This way everybody
can eat well and have fun.

13

Purim Gifts

At Purim, Jewish people give gifts to their friends and family members, too. This is another one of the four mitzvah they do during this holiday. They must give a gift to someone they know. The gifts are usually different foods such as nuts and baked goods.

This child and her father are delivering a gift to a friend.

● Nuts and baked goods are traditional Purim gifts.

The gift is called a **portion**. It must be a certain size. It cannot be too small or too large. This custom comes from the Story of Esther. These gifts celebrate friendship and being together.

DID YOU KNOW?

*Food gifts are to be **delivered** by someone other than the person who is giving. Often Jewish children are sent to deliver the gifts.*

15

The Purim Meal

Jewish people celebrate Purim by sharing a big meal. It is a happy time for family and friends to get together. During the meal, people tell jokes, sing, and have fun. They eat a lot!

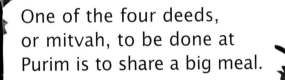

One of the four deeds, or mitvah, to be done at Purim is to share a big meal.

DID YOU KNOW?

The Purim meal starts on the afternoon of Purim and is carried on until sunset, when the holiday ends.

The Megillah tells Jewish people
to celebrate Purim with a feast.
The Purim meal is the last of
the four mitzvahs that should
be done on this day.

Meals shared with family and friends
are a happy part of Purim.

Traditional Purim Foods

Many Jewish people eat kosher foods only. Kosher is the Hebrew word for clean. Kosher foods are prepared, or made in a special way. A Purim feast has kosher foods.

Traditional Purim recipes for Hamantasch are passed down to grandchildren.

A traditional Purim food is Kreplach. It is a meat-filled dumpling. Nuts and seeds are eaten, too. In Queen Esther's story, she ate nuts and seeds while living at the king's palace. This is why they are eaten at Purim.

The meat is hidden in the traditional Purim dish, Kreplach.

DID YOU KNOW?

A favorite treat at Purim is Hamantasch. It is a triangle-shaped cookie filled with poppy-seed or prune filling. It looks like Haman's hat.

Dressing Up for Purim

On Purim, many children and even some adults dress up in costumes. It is a day to pretend to be somebody else.

Purim is a silly day when people hide who they are. In the Megillah, the idea of hiding comes up in a few different ways.

- Some Jewish children dress up as Queen Esther, or the other characters in Esther's story.

DID YOU KNOW?

At Purim, some Jews dress as people from Esther's story. Others dress up to be whoever or whatever they want to be. They can be Bart Simpson, Superman, or a butterfly.

20

You can be whoever or whatever you want to be during Purim.

First, Esther hid her Jewish background from the king. Second, people believed that even though God could not be seen, He helped the Jewish people. That is why people hide who they are by dressing up on Purim.

Purim Parades

People hold Purim parades to show off their costumes. Many dress up to go to synagogue to hear the Megillah. Some synagogues have a masquerade, or costume, parade afterward. They give prizes for the best costume.

Floats, such as this one, are a big part of the Purim parade in Holon, Israel.

Many people dress up in costumes for a Purim parade.

In Holon, Israel, a famous Purim parade is held every year. Many people dress in costumes for the parade. There are **floats** in some of the larger parades, too. Purim parades are called Adloyada. This is Hebrew for "do not know the other."

DID YOU KNOW?

*On Purim, some Jewish **communities** hold Queen-for-the-Day contests. The winner gets to be in a parade as Queen Esther.*

Having Fun on Purim

Purim is the happiest of Jewish holidays. People laugh and joke. They watch funny plays called Purim shpiels. These plays make fun of stories such as Esther's story.

Playing games during Purim is fun to do.

DID YOU KNOW?

One popular game at Purim is Burst Haman. People throw darts at balloons with Haman's face drawn on them. Players get a prize for breaking the balloon.

Some even do the play with puppets. Purim shpiels are held at synagogue parties and festivals during Purim.

People hold carnivals and festivals throughout the world. These are like big parties. People have fun. Sometimes there are entertainers to watch and games to play.

People put on plays and puppet shows that tell Esther's story.

Purim Songs

When happy people get together they like to sing songs. The Purim holiday has festive songs. Some were written long ago. Many were written in Hebrew and then changed into English and other languages. Some Purim songs tell Esther's story.

Happy children sing Purim songs on this holiday.

DID YOU KNOW?

Another popular Purim song is "Chag Purim." It is about laughing and singing and making noise with graggers.

Many Jewish children like the song, "Stomp, Stomp, Stomp." It is about Hamantaschen cookies shaped like Haman's hat. The song goes, "Stomp, stomp, stomp. Rat a tat tat. I'm going to eat your hat…"

Children learn and sing Purim songs at school, too!

27

Shushan Purim

In the Story of Esther, some Jewish people lived in a city with a wall around it called Shushan. There the fight against their enemies lasted for two days instead of one. Because of this, those Jewish people celebrated Purim one day later on the 15 of Adar. They called it Shushan Purim.

Jerusalem is an old city that had a wall around it. Part of this wall, shown here, still stands today.

Thousands of years ago, the holy city of Jerusalem, Israel, also had a wall around it. Today, people in Jerusalem and people who live in any city with a wall celebrate Shushan Purim.

Adults and children during Purim in Jerusalem.

DID YOU KNOW?

*Part of the **ancient** wall around Jerusalem still stands today. On Purim, Jewish people in Israel go to this wall to hear the Megillah.*

Purim Customs

To celebrate Purim, Jews perform the four deeds. They read the Megillah, give to charity, give to friends and family, and have a feast.

- Purim is a celebration when even rabbis can join in the fun.

DID YOU KNOW?

On Purim, some people write Haman on the bottoms of their shoes with chalk. During the Megillah reading, they stomp their feet to get rid of his name.

A custom long ago was to make something that represented Haman and then **destroy** it. Jews living in Germany, Italy, and Iran would burn a Haman doll at a Purim gathering. In colder places, such as Uzbekistan, there is snow at Purim. Jews would build a snowman and call it Haman. Then they would build a fire by the snowman and watch it melt.

Purim is one of the happiest of Jewish holidays!

31

Glossary

ancient Thousands of years old

calendar A system of days, weeks, and months that mark one year

charity To give to others in need

community A group of people with the same values or beliefs

deliver To bring something to someone else

destroy To ruin or wreck completely

feast A large, festive meal

float A stage that moves on wheels through a parade

holy Having to do with God

portion A certain amount, or share, of something

religious A person's belief in God

service A religious ceremony

sunset The time of day when the sun goes down and the nighttime follows

Index